All of M

Caroline Hc

methuen | drama

LONDON • NEW YORK • OXFORD • NEW DELHI • SYDNEY

METHUEN DRAMA
Bloomsbury Publishing Plc
50 Bedford Square, London, WC1B 3DP, UK
1385 Broadway, New York, NY 10018, USA

BLOOMSBURY, METHUEN DRAMA and the Methuen Drama logo are trademarks of Bloomsbury Publishing Plc

First published in Great Britain 2019

Cover design: Ben Anslow

Cover image © Holly Revell

A catalogue record for this book is available from the British Library.

A catalog record for this book is available from the Library of Congress.

ISBN: PB: 978-1-3501-5449-0
ePDF: 978-1-3501-5447-6
eBook: 978-1-3501-5448-3

Series: Modern Plays

Typeset by Mark Heslington Ltd, Scarborough, North Yorkshire
Printed and bound in Great Britain

To find out more about our authors and books visit www.bloomsbury.com and sign up for our newsletters.

All of Me

(the possibility of future splendour)

By Caroline Horton

Presented by Caroline Horton & Co. and China Plate, *All of Me* was first performed by Caroline Horton, directed by Alex Swift, at Summerhall at the Edinburgh Festival Fringe 2019, in a co-production with Cambridge Junction and The Yard Theatre where it received *The Scotsman* Mental Health Fringe Award 2019 and *The Stage* Edinburgh Award 2019.

All of Me transferred to The Yard Theatre in London in September 2019.

Commissioned by The Yard Theatre, Cambridge Junction, Harlow Playhouse, Birmingham Repertory Theatre, Theatr Iolo, ARC Stockton, The Brewhouse Arts Centre Burton, Camden People's Theatre and Folkestone Quarterhouse.

Supported by UCL Culture, Battersea Arts Centre, Artsdepot, mac Birmingham and In Good Company. Made in conversation with Birmingham Solihull Mental Health Trust and STOP Suicide (CPSL Mind).

Supported using public funding by the National Lottery through Arts Council England.

CREATIVE TEAM

Written and performed by Caroline Horton
Directed by Alex Swift

Designer | Eleanor Field
Lighting Designer | Katharine Williams
Sound Designer | Elena Peña
Associate Sound Designer | Charlotte Bickley
Composition | James Atherton
Songs | James Atherton & Caroline Horton
Dramaturg | Annie Siddons
Production Managers | Anthony Osborne & Jules Riley
Associate Director | Lucy Hopkins
Artist Wellbeing Practitioner | Lou Platt

Produced by China Plate

China Plate are:
Co-director | Ed Collier
Co-director | Paul Warwick
General Manager | Paul Hewlett
Senior Producer | Rosie Kelly
Producer | Tamara Moore
Producer | Susan Wareham
Engagement and Participation Producer | Andrea Pieri Gonzalez
Assistant Producer | Sammy Fiorino
Administrator | Sarah Isaacs

A special thanks to: The New Vic and Theresa Heskins, Valentina Ceschi, Stan's Café, Jill Norman, Positive Mental Health Group (Birmingham), Jacqueline Taylor, Professor Matthew Broome, Recovery College Birmingham's Anne Pledger and Steve Shaw, Alison Simpson, Professor Ulrike Schmidt, Dave and Clare O'Hara, Eve Fehilly, Dr Helen Sharpe, Dr Alexandra Pitman and Ed Jaspers.

Caroline Horton is a theatre maker, performer and writer. She was nominated for a 2013 Olivier Award for Outstanding Achievement in Affiliate Theatre for *You're Not Like The Other Girls Chrissy*, which won *The Stage* Awards Best Solo Performer in 2010. Other work for stage and radio includes *Mess* (Traverse Theatre, *The Stage* Awards Best Ensemble 2012), *Islands* (Bush Theatre), *Tranklements* (New Vic), *Penelope RETOLD* (Derby Theatre), *Paris, Nana & Me* and *Pandora* (BBC Radio 4) and *Muckers* (the egg, Theatre Royal Bath and Conde Duque, Madrid).

Caroline regularly collaborates with other companies as a deviser, performer, writer and director. She also mentors artists and companies and leads workshops. In 2016 she became the first BBC Birmingham Writer in Residence, and received a Collaborative Research Award from The Culture Capital Exchange. She was 2018/19 Creative Fellow at Birmingham University's Shakespeare Institute, teaching undergrad and MA students and developing work at The Other Place (RSC).

Alex Swift is a theatre maker, director and poet. Direction includes *How To Win Against History* by Seiriol Davies, *Mess* by Caroline Horton, *Heads Up* by Kieran Hurley, Luca Rutherford's *Political Party*, *Error 404* and *Instructions For Border Crossing* by Daniel Bye, and *Me & Mr C* by Gary Kitching.

Eleanor Field is a Theatre Designer and Artist, experienced in all styles of production, including collaborative and non-traditional theatre practice. Since graduating from RADA's Postgraduate Theatre Design course in July 2011, Eleanor has worked on projects across the UK.

Katharine Williams is a lighting designer for theatre, dance and music and has worked all over the world, including previous collaborations with Alex Swift and Caroline Horton. Katharine was lead artist on the Love Letters to the Home Office project and founder of the Crew for Calais initiative.

Elena Peña is a sound designer working in theatre, radio and installation. She collaborated with Caroline previously on *Islands* at the Bush Theatre. Recent work includes *Seven Methods of Killing Kylie Jenner* at the Royal Court, and upcoming projects include *Macbeth* at the Royal Exchange and *Snowflake* at the Kiln. Elena is an associate artist with Inspector Sands Theatre Company.

Charlotte Bickley is a composer, sound designer and DJ. Since cutting her teeth on various projects at Leeds Playhouse in early

2019, she's gone on to create the score and perform in Joana Nastari's award-winning *Fuck You Pay Me* at the Bunker, alongside playing live sets at festivals across Europe.

James Atherton has worked with some of the country's leading Arts organisations as a Musical Director and Composer for Television, Film and Theatre. James has worked with the Royal Opera House, English National Opera, Glyndbourne, Opera North, The New Vic Theatre, National Youth Music Theatre, Lion Television, Channel 4, ITV1, BBC1, BBC2, BBC4 and Film 4.

Annie Siddons is a writer, performer, dramaturg and comedian. Her show *How (not) to Live in Suburbia*, which sold out two runs at Soho, is being developed for TV. Her show *Dennis of Penge* returns to Soho in 2020. She is currently working on a new show, *Hybrid Emergency*, with Ursula Martinez.

Anthony Osbourne (Oz) has been a freelance stage, company and production manager for the last 22 years. He first got involved with a local youth theatre at the age of 13. He then spent many years running a transport business before being pulled back to his true passion.

Jules Riley has been an SM and DSM for a number of years, working on shows all over the UK and abroad. Most recently she has been touring with a show called *Muckers*, which was written by Caroline Horton and produced by the egg and Theatre Royal Bath. Jules has very much enjoyed being part of the team for *All Of Me* while covering for their Production Manager.

Lucy Hopkins is an award-winning, internationally-touring clown, director, creative consultant, activist priestess, workshop leader and clever person. The foundation of all of her work is her full-hearted belief that people are tremendous.

Lou Platt is an Artist Wellbeing Practitioner who works with artists (individuals, creative teams and companies) to care for and enhance their mental health when they're in relationship to their art. Lou is a dramatherapist, clinical supervisor and theatre practitioner and has been pioneering this practice since 2012.

FOREWORD

This show was developed from a place of hopelessness.

Now it's made, I think it is hopeful (and dark as fuck) but hopeful nonetheless. But that's just my opinion.

Like many (probably all?) theatre pieces, *All of Me* is a lot more than these words – it's built of sounds, music, images, games … but that's ok and I'm really grateful to have it here in a book.

I started work on it in 2016, dredging the depths to find out what (if anything) I had to say. In collaboration with brilliant directors and designers, improvising and writing, writing and improvising, it (very slowly) found its way to Edinburgh in 2019 via various hair-raising work-in-progress performances. Sorry and thank you to those audiences.

Although autobiographical, the show was also informed by conversations with people about their experiences of living with or treating addiction, depression, eating disorders or suicidal ideation. And about their experiences of recovery – about all the things recovery can mean.

Of course, *All of Me* is about depression (or about my particular version of that diagnosable condition) but beyond that highly personal experience of mental illness, it is also political. I feel like the anxiety, or exhaustion, or deep despair that so many of us share is asking us to refuse or rebel in a relentless world, where growth and progress supersede care and space to breathe.

I will always be grateful for the experience of making this piece, and especially to Alex Swift for his brilliance, his understanding of the deep dark and his friendship for the last twenty years.

Caroline Horton

www.carolinehorton.net

China Plate works with artists, venues, festivals and funders to develop, make and present engaging, adventurous and accessible new work.

Launched by Ed Collier and Paul Warwick in 2006, China Plate is passionate about creating adventurous and imaginative new work with popular appeal and a social purpose. Using theatre to engage and inspire, the company takes work into theatres, village halls, schools, onto the streets and to festivals in the UK and internationally.

In 2018/19, China Plate created, toured and programmed work for 35,000 people across 148 venues (nationally and internationally), with a diverse programme of shows and events. It produces innovative development programmes including The Darkroom, Next Stages, The Optimists (producer training), and the First Bite and Bite Size festivals.

China Plate is an Associate Producer at Warwick Arts Centre.

China Plate is a National Portfolio Organisation supported using public funds by Arts Council England.

www.chinaplatetheatre.com

CAMBRIDGE JUNCTION

Cambridge Junction is the arts centre in Cambridge where art meets life.

Since opening its doors on the former site of the city's cattle market in 1990, Cambridge Junction has been a hub for people to come together, explore and be inspired by the arts, entertainment and creative learning. Each year over 100,000 people visit for 400 performances across three spaces.

Cambridge Junction presents a renowned and diverse programme of theatre, dance, popular culture and family events as well as supporting and fostering new artistic talent and working with young people from across the region.

Cambridge Junction is a social enterprise, earning over 50% of its income through events and activities which is reinvested back into the business and its social mission.

'*With an excellent booking policy, good facilities and friendly staff, Cambridge Junction is certainly a jewel in the east of England's crown.*' The Guardian

Cambridge Junction is a National Portfolio Organisation supported using public funds by Arts Council England.

www.junction.co.uk

Built in a disused warehouse by a group of volunteers in 2011, The Yard is now a vital part of London's arts landscape. The Yard is a place for explosive new theatre. It produces bold, politically-charged stories from the edges of our society, in a way that is unapologetically live. Over recent years The Yard has produced a wide range of highly-acclaimed shows, from *This Beautiful Future* (★★★★★ 'Mesmerising' – *The Stage*) to *The Crucible* (★★★★★ 'Without doubt, the finest production of *The Crucible* I have ever seen' – *Evening Standard*).

The Yard is one of London's most exciting venues for experiencing music, hosting parties organised by and for under-represented groups in London's music scene. Working with both internationally-renowned and new collectives, The Yard hosts over 100 music events each year. The Yard also offers a local programme which ensures that young people have access to the arts. It manages two community centres in the local area to deliver innovative, creative activity for local residents.

The Yard is a National Portfolio Organisation supported using public funds by Arts Council England.

theyardtheatre.co.uk

All of Me

A mix-tape of bad songs, each titled 'All of Me' plays as the audience enters.

Onstage is a scaff tower with rough wooden planks across it, there seems to be an orchid on a small shelf. Bits of clothing are strewn about. Three hessian sandbags hang on ropes. A smaller scaff structure is covered in bits of technical kit, including a couple of computer screens. There are angle-poise lamps on the main scaff tower and across the front of the stage. There is cable everywhere. Three mirror balls have been dumped on the floor downstage.

When she enters, she looks at the audience and leaves. She re-appears. This is not an apology. She wears old shorts, slippers with socks, and a ripped sequined jacket. She ambles about, and quite a lot of this is shouted.

Hello.

I'd like to apologise for what happens next.

I apologise if it doesn't live up to your expectations of theatre or art.

I apologise for not having tried to cover up its shortcomings with skill – such as tap-dancing – I can't dance – though at one point I did begin with tap-dancing.

There aren't even interesting or inventive uses of technology – don't let the computer screens and all the cable raise any expectations of that sort – they're from a previous version of the show.

I apologise too for the heavy subject matter. I at least hope this isn't a surprise – I did mention dying on the flyer. But I'm sorry if you didn't get a flyer or if you have ended up in here by accident and now feel trapped in a show where the performer already seems to have gone off piste.

I actually haven't – gone off piste. I apologise if knowing that this is planned makes you feel worse.

I apologise for not surprising you with a light show about depression and death – it's going to remain quite a dark show about those dark things. In March I called the show's producer and said I was sorry for not being able to work, not returning emails and refusing to engage with the world because I was once again depressed and suicidal and regularly eating my own weight in granola and cake mix. After an awkward silence – a bit like this one – he was nice about it and in that phone call I said I wanted the show to have more jokes – that as I was going to be doing it in Edinburgh for a month and then in London for another month – it'd be better for everyone if it wasn't unrelentingly bleak. It was a genuine desire (and he seemed relieved) but I'd like to apologise because it hasn't materialised – there aren't more jokes.

I apologise that despite trying for three and a half years to make something formally groundbreaking that would authentically capture my experience of what some people call 'mental illness', I have in fact ended up telling a story – with a beginning and a middle and an end – and it's not even a new story – I have rehashed a myth and then made it fit into a 70-minute Edinburgh slot.

She turns her back and rests her head on the tower.

I apologise for not being at my best – for not offering you my best self or even a professional façade. This show is the way it is because I am tired – in lots of ways – mostly of tidying myself up – and of hiding stuff – for example, the frequent sensation of not wanting to be alive or of being too scared to get up in the mornings slash afternoons – but more of that later.

Clearly today I've succeeded in getting out of bed (though this may be due to my ingrained obedience). Had things still been really bad I wouldn't be here – onstage – and I wouldn't be apologising. So I apologise for being neither ready for this, nor unready enough to have stayed in bed.

I am also sorry you have had to pay a lot of money to be here – if it helps at all – so have I – we are all on the same ugly cruise ship built by megalomaniac rich people telling us that art is important and we are all having a truly wonderful time.

I apologise for not doing proper marketing and obeying deadlines. I know this has made various people's lives more difficult, mainly the people whose job it has been to sell this show. It is very resistant to being for sale.

I'm sorry too for asking the fringe brochure to cross out the show's title. I'm also sorry that they refused. And further to that, I apologise to anyone here who thought they were getting all of me – you're not. The title (as I have mentioned) is in fact 'All of Me' crossed out – but apparently crossing things out is confusing for people and press and brochures.

She triggers a loud hopeful music track then immediately stops it.

I apologise for making yet another show about me. If a different character does appear, it is probably just another version of me – don't get your hopes up.

She takes a chair from a stack in the wings and sits.

I know some people feel concerned about this growing tendency to 'hang dirty laundry out in public pretending that it's art', and they feel very clear that this activity 'belongs in therapy and not on the stage'. I apologise if you are one of them – you'll really hate this.

I should also apologise for again adding to the long list of fringe shows about depression slash eating disorders slash other mental illnesses. Maybe the way to stop every other show being about mental illness would be to un-fuck the world?

I'm sorry for making a show from whose material I have no healthy distance – none. I know this has caused various people a lot of worry – I have found it interesting. Though I apologise if I do cry or briefly leave the stage – I won't be acting – I cannot cry on demand (another skill I won't be offering) – I'll just be sorting through my shit.

Lastly I apologise for not doing the show as carefully rehearsed and designed last year – and as sold to this venue. This is the set for that previous version – the one that I'm not doing. As you now know I got ill again this year, so the version I made when I was well and productive and showering and changing my underwear – was far too uplifting.

So about 6 weeks ago I ruined that show. For you. Very carefully.

So here – at the start – I wasn't going to apologise – everyone knows you shouldn't apologise at the start of a show – it makes the audience uncomfortable. Sorry.

No, I was going to do a glitter drop – like this – (*she releases a rope from the small scaff tower and a surprisingly large amount of glitter falls on her head*) – whilst pretending to feel hopeless, with the glitter drop symbolising how theatre (symbolising how life) wasn't really working for me anymore. Anyway, this all involved a lot of pretending (or acting) which I'm currently finding tiring and pointless, so I'm not doing that.

She looks at the audience and decides what she needs.

(*On microphone.*) Shall we go to the beach? I like the beach.

She sets up sound effects to create a beach scene on the loop station. First the sound of waves with her breath, then a gentle wind, a few gulls overhead . . . a small dog runs about by the waves, a child asks for an ice cream. It wasn't going to stay nice for long. Gulls scream and dive-bomb her, someone yells that they've found a condom, the 'cute' dog attacks her, police sirens speed along the road, a seagull shits on the kid's ice cream, someone is screaming that the water is freezing. She turns up the volume. When it's been unbearable for long enough, she silences the loop.

(*On microphone.*) I should probably just get on with it.

She adjusts a desklamp to light herself at the music station, then turns on the record player and creates a loop of the scratching sound.

Prologue. (*She crosses to the chair downstage right.*) Ok – this is the start of the myth.

She had been crawling on her belly for some time across the broken glass when she stopped. She couldn't be arsed. The going had been slow, and despite using her arms relatively effectively like a crocodile or a lizard, because she is not any of these creatures, she stopped. She nibbles on some dead raisins she finds in the bottom of her handbag. She doesn't hear her sister's voice calling from somewhere far below. It starts to rain, so she drags her body into the doorway of the nearest building – an uninspiring community centre. Through the glass she watches contented faces pottering about. They settle into a circle. One of them with boring hair spots her and beckons. She crawls on her belly into the warm. They pull another chair into the circle and she hides underneath it. She lies there listening to their stories – their broken soul stories. Love is there. She's always found love. She opens her mouth to speak but, lizard-like, no sound. Boring Hair smiles encouragingly and Lizard – always eager to please – tries once more.

She stands, leaving the microphone on the chair, then drags on a music stand with a copy of the text taped onto a bit of cardboard. She half-sings the text.

Hello   I thought I'd introduce myself properly   as is polite

My name is Caroline Horton. I'm 37 years old. I live near Coventry.

I was born in Lichfield, Staffordshire, on a Tuesday. Our house was in a nice cul de sac. My parents are accountants.

I'm married to Ed. He's 40 years old with brown hair, glasses, a teacher, etc.

I have no children but I wish I had a dog – a big dog.

I am a vegan except when I want milk in my coffee and there's no soya.

I like drinking red wine especially with salted peanuts especially in pubs.

I love bluebells in forests in May.

I love going to the cinema during the day – alone.

I love dancing – I mean really dancing – I want to dance til I'm dripping and all I can smell is human bodies sweating and my feet hurt.

I love getting drunk, so drunk I can't remember a lot of what happened and I wake up in the morning feeling so disgusting then saying 'Fuck it – today's a write off. Yeah. Today's a write off'. I have a crack in the front of my skull from one such night.

Did I say I love dancing? It makes me happy and so does sex, but not always.

What else? Floodlights. Mirror balls. Going to bed at times when you're not meant to go to bed. Breaking china.

I love holidays and I might take an inappropriately long one soon.

I love staying up really late really too late and feeling like the world is asleep and missing out.

I love sunrises but not with someone annoying.

I love singing mournful songs and wine with peanuts and the smell of armpits.

I want to speak at least five languages brilliantly and write a novel and have it acclaimed and grow really old but the older I get the more fabulous I feel and get enlightened and analysed and learn to play the piano and the trumpet and sing like Billie Holiday and dance like Fred Astaire and swear like a bastard who doesn't care.

I love – in love – I love – even as I peel and stink and weep and bruise and leak – I am shouting – I am sweaty dying decaying – I'm a woman more or less – with armpits and big feet and greying hair that I sometimes remember to dye – I think about dying a lot . . . the other sort of dying . . .

When Darkness lands like a motherfucker with teeth bared and brains poking through her skull saying she wants to lie with me skin to skin – skin to skin – and sometimes I want to lie with her too but not all the time – she doesn't call ahead.

I dream of slipping away but I know it won't be slipping it'll be bloody and/or painful. I imagine the funeral and feel guilty for the loved ones, but not for long because everybody dies – everybody's body is falling apart in front of our eyes – our minds are disintegrating – I wish I still smoked – I loved smoking before breakfast especially – I won't go for that smear test that'll do it – the cells are mutating probably as I speak – at traffic lights I creep over the edge over the painted white line – imagine being knocked off my bike which would look like an accident and doing everything for the last time – last time I had a big spoonful of trifle on my way to the pills – it was delicious but not delicious enough.

Hello   I thought I'd introduce myself properly   as is polite

She returns the music stand, sits and speaks on mic.

Some of them nod, Boring Hair takes a sip of her tea, then more stories. When it is done, Lizard leaves, with no idea of going back, carrying their pamphlet home in her teeth.

She triggers a deep rumbling sound from the launchpad on the music station. The microphone voice shifts – it's deep, distorted, it's her Shadow-sister from the underworld.

Sister! Hey Princess! Stop pretending you can't hear me – I'm really loud. Get down here! I'm your sister remember.

She adds a gentle kalimba line to the record crackle on the loop, and then a soft sung line.

Dark night. Dark since late July. Age 99 years a stooped body bangs about a small house. Out of vodka it pushes pyjamas into wellies and coat and shuffles to the car. Tesco's bright letters cut through the winter gloom. Plastic-packed muffins, cheesecake, red wine, Maltesers – fun size. Anonymous up and down the aisles with its unwashed hair. It hasn't spoken all day and chooses the automated check-out but a human appears to authorise the wine, the vodka. Stony-faced at the request for ID, it hands over a driving licence muttering 'I am a hundred years old'. Safe home it pours stiff drinks, turns up Netflix to drown out her sister's shouting, and recommences obliteration.

She cuts the loop. She sets the loop going as she sings, harmonies building and building until the song reaches a relentless crescendo.

Keep calm and carry on
Keep calm and drink your tea
Keep calm and stay smiling
Keep calm and carry on and on and on and on

Keep calm and eat chocolate
Keep calm and smoke a fag
Keep calm and go out shopping
Keep calm and carry on and on and
on and on and on and on and on and
on and on and on and on and on

Keep calm and work together
Keep calm and hold your breath
Keep calm and think of England
Keep calm and carry on and on and
on and on and on and on and on and
on and on and on and on and on and
on and on and on and on and on and
on and on and on and on and on and
on and on and on

She cuts the loop, and builds a gentle birdsong loop. She kneels.

Standing in the back garden, swollen under the winter sun, face upwards. She prays. And again. She neither laughs nor mocks. For an agnostic she finds she is in fact extremely willing – to pray. She feels something in her dressing-gown pocket – a folded pamphlet talking about redemption. She heads inside, stands at the turning point, then lies down on the kitchen floor. And from somewhere far, far below she hears her sister's song.

She lays her jacket down revealing an oversized t-shirt with Death written across the front. She triggers the track.

Shadow-sister microphone voice. Are you listening yet Princess?

She throws a huge white skirt made of parachute silk over her head and puts on Shadow-sister's headdress made of feathers and an animal skull. She wields the haze machine about, creating Shadow-sister's image. She sings from upstage.

Let me tell you about pain
How it sits on your chest – it's sitting tight
Sitting pretty.
Let me tell you about pain
How it holds you still – ever so still
You're still breathing.

No point in freaking out
Just put on your shoes and dance it out
No point in freaking out
Just put on your shoes and dance it out

Let me tell you about pain
How it promises to stay
Voice like oil – you know its voice.
Let me tell you about pain
You heard it approach – you felt it knocking
You opened the door

No point in freaking out
Just put on your shoes and dance it out
No point in freaking out
Just put on your shoes and dance it out

She walks slowly downstage, removes the headdress.

Let me tell you about pain
It comes when you forget
Let me tell you about pain
I remind you of pain

She melts to the floor, removing the skirt. She speaks on microphone.

Another character – not me – opens the kitchen door.

Hello . . . What are you doing on the floor? . . . I bought you apples. Do you fancy an apple? . . . What's the plan Stan? . . .

Things aren't right. Deep down. Down in the underworld. My sister's beside herself. I've left her alone there too long. I must attend the rites.

Shall I come?

I will go alone. I am to put on my best robes – my crown – carry my measure in my hand.

Does this mean you're having a shower?

No.

Can I ask who am I in all this?

My faithful handmaiden.

Your handmaiden?

Faithfully awaiting my return. Yeah – things may get dirty in the underworld.

Ok . . . well, I'll run you a bath.

She adds a distant call to the loop as she collects the moon from upstage right. She holds the moon close to her face.

She begins to walk – with slow stupid steps. The sand slows her feet. The voices in her head slow too – like a tape chewing itself up. There are twelve gates before she reaches her sister's palace. At the first she has a fight because the gatekeeper's a bitch and steals her crown. At the second she finds a bar selling cheap red wine . . . so naturally she doesn't remember the rest. When she awakes, she is naked at the door of the underworld. Years older. Cleaned out. Her eyes have dried out and one of them falls to the floor. She watches her sister's white spiders clamber across her feet in the moonlight – their strange translucent bodies marrying with the white sand.

She turns the moon off, stops the loop and the stage snaps to sudden bright light.

At this point – I used to take my clothes off – all of them. Anyway, back at the door to the underworld she gives Handmaiden a call – you can imagine the nakedness if it feels germane.

She stands upstage and sings to the upper world – the sound is huge, breaking.

Brrr Brrr Brrr Brrr
Hey – hello – it's only me.
I'm not going to make it for dinner tonight.
Sorry for the short notice.
Sorry for the rambling voicemail.

She triggers the sound of the underworld, and the microphone voice is that of her Shadow-sister. She slowly adjusts the angle-poise lamps on the large scaff tower to point upwards.

Hello. Want something?
What about what I want?
What about what I desire?

She clambers up onto the scaff tower and pulls on Shadow-sister's huge black skirt. She takes off her t-shirt. She stands half-naked and puts on the headdress. She makes sure she is properly lit.

Welcome to my kingdom. So this sister of mine – she finally paid me a visit, after all these years. We'll go from her entrance. Ta da!!

Well, here you are then Princess (she hates it when I call her that) so Princess, what took you so long? I've missed you –

have you missed me? She says 'Can she have her clothes back, her crown?' I say 'No . . . no need' and I reach my hand around her little neck. Her little limbs shoot out sideways like a kitten not used to being picked up. I like cats. I keep squeezing – lift her whole body up to watch the limbs flicker.

She pierces the central sandbag – sand pours down. She crouches, watching the life drain.

When she's still and dangly like a dangly thing – I hang her on a peg – like a coat – a duffle coat for example. Very sad. But what could I do when push came to shove? She should have come when I called.

She sits and triggers a new, more melancholic sound.

Three days later when our lovely Princess is drained of blood like a pasty piggy in a butcher's shop, I decide I want to go out (*She puts on a short silver jacket with Death written in sequins on the back.*) – stretch my legs – go wild – grief needs that sometimes. I carry her carcass through the city of the dead, under orange blossom and neon signs, towards the disco lights of my favourite bar.

She triggers her bar music and then orchestrates shifts and builds within it.

I love this one. Romantic. Something else. No – something else. Contemporary. No. It's not enough.

She descends, prowls about, piercing the other two sandbags as the bar sounds build and grow chaotic.

It's not enough. No. Louder! I prop Princess up on a white leather sofa. She slumps. Her head keeps smacking onto the table. (*She looks up at the central sandbag pouring sand.*) 'Princess I want you to dance. Why won't you dance with me? You always leave me on my own.' Look – I brought you something.

She turns on the Jolly Penguin Race toy – then stops the bar sounds – only the music from the penguins plays as they climb the stairs and slide back down the slide . . . She begins mostly on the microphone in the Shadow-sister voice, then gradually speaking directly to the audience off-mic.

Do you remember this? This is the Jolly Penguin Race. You bought it in a shopping centre in Cheltenham. You'd watch it for hours. You said it calmed you down. The worst thing is the music and the flashing lights and the little flags that tell the penguins it's so great – it's so fun. But it's not.

We should be terrified. Some people get panic attacks in shopping centres. I mean, why aren't we all getting panic attacks in shopping centres? Have you been to a shopping centre lately? We should all be getting panic attacks in shopping centres if there was any sense to be made. And what about the people who are militantly ok? How are they so ok? They don't have panic attacks in shopping centres. And why do they always seem to be the ones in charge? 'Climb the stairs' they say 'Bravo! You're at the top – bravo! Now what? Oh now you go back down again – bravo! And again – bravo! Until your batteries run out and we bury you in the ground – bravo! Bury you, your shell, in the ground – bravo!'

She turns the penguins off.

Why don't we stop? Why don't we ask why? Who for? Says who?

Fear. Fear sits upon the throne where she should never sit, sits burping, squirming, she had a white-knuckle grip on my sister's heart. Had you kept me closer – your shadow, your soul, your depth, your plunging depths, your freedom, your foul, your negative, your darkness – I'd have waged war for you. But you stopped coming over to play – you shouldn't have left my desert behind Princess – my city in the desert – the void the vast void.

And these days deserts are few and far between – they are precious. We fill them up – cramming them with shit – we plug them – our space – spaces – with junk plastic habits patterns noise distractions – to numb re-numb renew-the-numb again and again. For it is terrifying to lay down with emptiness – to soak in nothingness – accepting – surrendering to the vast splendour of space – space where we are sure to feel something, know something, feel something rolling through us, tumbling through us, melting something within us – from our deep gut selves, deep soul selves, deep natures, our life death life natures, our godly dirty same as every other sacred being natures.

All this has been said before but it bears repeating – and if you'd listened Princess – if you would listen – I wouldn't need to kill you.

'Can't you make small talk?' She'd say 'Have a polite conversation? Where's the funny bit? I need some entertainment. I'm thinking of having a kid – I maybe want a kid – something else to fill up this . . .'

This what? This void? Can we not allow the void to speak, to become eloquent? Let it be what it is. The world is not reasonable it is unreasonable; it is not rational it is irrational; it is not clear it is unclear – despite our longings for reason, for clarity, our desperate moulding of chaos into something masquerading as meaning, story, even redemption . . .

All this has been said before but we forget, we forget, we are the most forgetful creatures. We forget how to stand in the desert – we tell ourselves we cannot stand it. Sit with me amongst these rocks because who are we racing for? Obeying for? When soon we will be no one, and nowhere.

You've gone quiet but I am incredibly loud.

And I want to talk. I want to talk of fear and souls and cages and gods. How death is coming so what to do – how to live in its face. How to stand the desert – the void – flourish even – even flourish – with the cacti and the succulents – to bloom.

To ask quietly earnestly 'Where are our gods?' Cos oh oh oh we could do with one or two right now I reckon. Or if not gods then god-shaped holes – our souls. Let us make space in the world for our god-shaped holes. For we are holy – we are so holy.

And there is another order – another law – another way – another time besides jolly penguin time. There's ocean time, wild time, enough-time time, there's mountain time, dark when it's dark time, light when it's light time, time with spaces time, time with time enough to breathe, there's breath-time, instead of the race to the end time.

And inside the hopelessness of the void, inside the asking how to come out of the suffering, out of the smallness the smallness the suffering. A hope. Because there's hope and then there's hope. And life is thick with hopeless darkness, it knocks us flying, my sister grew weak with it. Our griefs, they flow in rivers through us – the source unquenchable but how incredible – to have rivers running through us – even rivers of grief. Hollowing out channels in the stone of us, carving us, sculpting us, drawing lines across our foreheads.

And how do we live with the void how do we live with the void how do we live with death how do we live with the void?

Eventually – at long last – like most all the jolly penguins in all the world – we tire – we reach the end of our tethers. Hallejulah. Exhaustion and despair they are our friends, I swear they are our friends. Hallejulah. And all greatness all hope can begin from this place. Into this space creeps some moonlight, into this crack that has opened. And here we can begin . . . to refuse – refuse shame, refuse smallness, refuse story, refuse work, refuse manners, refuse to be quiet, refuse to behave, refuse to succeed. We can lie down with Refusal. Can fail, learn, accept, surrender. Fail more profoundly still. Wait a bit. Wait. We'll wait til we're fucking ready.

She removes the headdress.

Just before the end you didn't want to die. Why Princess? What does it possibly mean? When apparently life is suffering suffering smallness and suffering. It must mean that that's not all there is.

I understand suicide. We can all understand suicide despite our reticence. Suicide – an understandable confession that life's too much – an understandable confession that it's not worth the trouble.

But what if – what if we can surrender . . . surrender to the vast deep dark of the desert plains? Can we recover maybe? Recover ourselves over and over. Re-fuck it up. Re-surrender. Re-recover. Spiralling slowly painstakingly incrementally towards soul . . . towards peace of a sort.

You said you'd lost joy – I said 'Well where's it gone? When did you last have it sister? I can get it back for you if you persist – if you can persist. And I promise it won't always feel this hard.'

(*Back into the microphone, in Shadow-sister's voice.*) Let's look out across the desert – across the void – look there's beauty in the darkness in the dread – messages. Look out across the vastness – feel small – absurd – temporary – free. Wait there – there – I'll send up a flare. Illuminate it for you a second – just a second – the void – vast void. Wait, leave the lights off.

She gets changed – removes the huge black skirt and puts on a new t-shirt, it also has Death written on the front. She carries the loop pedal downstage and sits by the sand. She sets up a gentle beach loop. She speaks into the microphone.

The sisters lie together under the covers – one is a corpse and the other's her shadow from the underworld – and they sleep and sleep – and they don't know if they're in the land of the living or the city of the dead, or if it's morning or night or lunchtime or 4am. Time has disintegrated and they don't give a shit.

There's no language.

Handmaiden appears with hot water bottles and cups of decaf tea.

At some point, Handmaiden drives the corpse to the GP, returning with drugs and a leaflet about self-referral. Then the weeks pass until the pills kick in.

One day the corpse shuffles to the bathroom, where her shadow peels off layers of damp clothes that smell of armpits. Under the shower the corpse uncoils – just a little. The rest of the day she can't stop touching her clean hair that smells of coconut shampoo.

More sleeping.

One afternoon, the sisters sit outside in the grey June drizzle.

She alternates between the different microphone voices as the sisters talk.

Should I thank you for strangling me?

And for putting you back together.

My head's wonky.

It'll help you remember me. Forget me again and I'll ruin you.

Right.

And keep your spare room free.

Will you call ahead?

No.

Ok – maybe we could write sometimes? I'll email.

I'll fucking haunt you.

Got it.

She half-sings, off-mic.

I look up
I look at the sky
I look at the colour – more than one colour . . .

Try to hold the day precious day in the cup of my hands, wondrous hands.
What if I can only drag bones?
What if the morning light you rave on about has no splendour?
What if the world is badly lit?

The lights snap up bright and warm. She squints and stands up.

That's the end of the myth.

She asks the audience on mic.

Shall we imagine a party?

She triggers the party track that builds and flows, it's rich and layered and beautiful.

So who've we got? Oh they're all here.

She turns the angle-poise lamps out front one by one and sits with the audience to watch the party.

There's Death – the gawky teenager with dip-dyed hair (she fancies Joy) and Wild One is sat on the table, naked with muddy feet grinning at Rage. Desire's playing drinking games with True Love, and Peace is dancing with Beauty, who is having a sordid affair with Ugliness. Exhaustion's stroking Fear's knee under the table and she likes it. Success and Failure are out in the corridor – they're arguing about who's having the kids on Saturday. Shame is late – he's in a meeting with Judgment that overran and until he shows up . . . Hope's telling jokes and pouring shots for anyone who'll listen and generally trying to fit in. Ugliness is sick of Beauty ignoring her – she's taking Wild One out to the garden for a fag and maybe something more. The dark garden is long and broad – it's good for wandering – patches of woodland, soft green lawns and further still the cliffs and the sound of the sea. The lights from the house spill out and the party rolls on late.

The beat crashes in and the lights dance as she sings.

Hold your own my darling
Hold firm – your roots are growing
Hold up your head my darling
Hold true to me I'll hold to you

Hold true to all the gods in you
Hold close the good and bad of you
Hold land and sea in you
Hold all your gods in you

Hold out for all that we miss
Hold on in the dark
Hold morning skies in you
Hold all the night in you

The music fades, we hear again the gentle loop of the waves.

I'll stop here for now. And it won't always feel like this (*she allows this text to build and loop as she leaves the stage*) and then it will again and then it won't again and then it will again and then it won't again . . . and sometimes the sky will be lighter, and sometimes darker, and then lighter again, and then darker again and sometimes I'll be above ground and sometimes below ground and then it'll be lighter again, and then darker again, then lighter again, then darker again . . .

She leaves the stage, the loop continues to build.

The lights and sound surge briefly then silence, blackout.

Methuen Drama
Classical Greek Dramatists

Aeschylus Plays: One
(Persians, Seven Against Thebes, Suppliants, Prometheus Bound)

Aeschylus Plays: Two
(Oresteia: Agamemnon, Libation-Bearers, Eumenides)

Aristophanes Plays: One
(Acharnians, Knights, Peace, Lysistrata)

Aristophanes Plays: Two
(Wasps, Clouds, Birds, Festival Time, Frogs)

Aristophanes & Menander: New Comedy
(Women in Power, Wealth, The Malcontent, The Woman from Samos)

Euripides Plays: One
(Medea, The Phoenician Women, Bacchae)

Euripides Plays: Two
(Hecuba, The Women of Troy, Iphigeneia at Aulis, Cyclops)

Euripides Plays: Three
(Alkestis, Helen, Ion)

Euripides Plays: Four
(Elektra, Orestes, Iphigeneia in Tauris)

Euripides Plays: Five
(Andromache, Herakles' Children, Herakles)

Euripides Plays: Six
(Hippolytos, Suppliants, Rhesos)

Sophocles Plays: One
(Oedipus the King, Oedipus at Colonus, Antigone)

Sophocles Plays: Two
(Ajax, Women of Trachis, Electra, Philoctetes)

Methuen Drama Contemporary Dramatists

include

John Arden (two volumes)
Arden & D'Arcy
Peter Barnes (three volumes)
Sebastian Barry
Mike Bartlett
Dermot Bolger
Edward Bond (ten volumes)
Howard Brenton (two volumes)
Leo Butler (two volumes)
Richard Cameron
Jim Cartwright
Caryl Churchill (two volumes)
Complicite
Sarah Daniels (two volumes)
Nick Darke
David Edgar (three volumes)
David Eldridge (two volumes)
Ben Elton
Per Olov Enquist
Dario Fo (two volumes)
Michael Frayn (four volumes)
John Godber (four volumes)
Paul Godfrey
James Graham (two volumes)
David Greig
John Guare
Lee Hall (two volumes)
Katori Hall
Peter Handke
Jonathan Harvey (two volumes)
Iain Heggie
Israel Horovitz
Declan Hughes
Terry Johnson (three volumes)
Sarah Kane
Barrie Keeffe
Bernard-Marie Koltès (two volumes)
Franz Xaver Kroetz
Kwame Kwei-Armah
David Lan
Bryony Lavery
Deborah Levy
Doug Lucie
David Mamet (four volumes)
Patrick Marber
Martin McDonagh
Duncan McLean
David Mercer (two volumes)
Anthony Minghella (two volumes)
Tom Murphy (six volumes)
Phyllis Nagy
Anthony Neilson (two volumes)
Peter Nichol (two volumes)
Philip Osment
Gary Owen
Louise Page
Stewart Parker (two volumes)
Joe Penhall (two volumes)
Stephen Poliakoff (three volumes)
David Rabe (two volumes)
Mark Ravenhill (three volumes)
Christina Reid
Philip Ridley (two volumes)
Willy Russell
Eric-Emmanuel Schmitt
Ntozake Shange
Sam Shepard (two volumes)
Martin Sherman (two volumes)
Christopher Shinn (two volumes)
Joshua Sobel
Wole Soyinka (two volumes)
Simon Stephens (three volumes)
Shelagh Stephenson
David Storey (three volumes)
C. P. Taylor
Sue Townsend
Judy Upton
Michel Vinaver (two volumes)
Arnold Wesker (two volumes)
Peter Whelan
Michael Wilcox
Roy Williams (four volumes)
David Williamson
Snoo Wilson (two volumes)
David Wood (two volumes)
Victoria Wood

Methuen Drama Modern Plays
include work by

Bola Agbaje
Edward Albee
Davey Anderson
Jean Anouilh
John Arden
Peter Barnes
Sebastian Barry
Alistair Beaton
Brendan Behan
Edward Bond
William Boyd
Bertolt Brecht
Howard Brenton
Amelia Bullmore
Anthony Burgess
Leo Butler
Jim Cartwright
Lolita Chakrabarti
Caryl Churchill
Lucinda Coxon
Curious Directive
Nick Darke
Shelagh Delaney
Ishy Din
Claire Dowie
David Edgar
David Eldridge
Dario Fo
Michael Frayn
John Godber
Paul Godfrey
James Graham
David Greig
John Guare
Mark Haddon
Peter Handke
David Harrower
Jonathan Harvey
Iain Heggie
Robert Holman
Caroline Horton
Terry Johnson
Sarah Kane
Barrie Keeffe
Doug Lucie
Anders Lustgarten
David Mamet
Patrick Marber
Martin McDonagh
Arthur Miller
D. C. Moore
Tom Murphy
Phyllis Nagy
Anthony Neilson
Peter Nichols
Joe Orton
Joe Penhall
Luigi Pirandello
Stephen Poliakoff
Lucy Prebble
Peter Quilter
Mark Ravenhill
Philip Ridley
Willy Russell
Jean-Paul Sartre
Sam Shepard
Martin Sherman
Wole Soyinka
Simon Stephens
Peter Straughan
Kate Tempest
Theatre Workshop
Judy Upton
Timberlake Wertenbaker
Roy Williams
Snoo Wilson
Frances Ya-Chu Cowhig
Benjamin Zephaniah

Methuen Drama Student Editions

Jean Anouilh *Antigone* • John Arden *Serjeant Musgrave's Dance* • Alan Ayckbourn *Confusions* • Aphra Behn *The Rover* • Edward Bond *Lear* • *Saved* • Bertolt Brecht *The Caucasian Chalk Circle* • *Fear and Misery in the Third Reich* • *The Good Person of Szechwan* • *Life of Galileo* • *Mother Courage and Her Children* • *The Resistible Rise of Arturo Ui* • *The Threepenny Opera* • Anton Chekhov *The Cherry Orchard* • *The Seagull* • *Three Sisters* • *Uncle Vanya* • Caryl Churchill *Serious Money* • *Top Girls* • Shelagh Delaney *A Taste of Honey* • Euripides *Elektra* • *Medea* • Dario Fo *Accidental Death of an Anarchist* • Michael Frayn *Copenhagen* • John Galsworthy *Strife* • Nikolai Gogol *The Government Inspector* • Carlo Goldoni *A Servant to Two Masters* • Lorraine Hansberry *A Raisin in the Sun* • Robert Holman *Across Oka* • Henrik Ibsen *A Doll's House* • *Ghosts* • *Hedda Gabler* • Sarah Kane *4.48 Psychosis* • *Blasted* • Charlotte Keatley *My Mother Said I Never Should* • Bernard Kops *Dreams of Anne Frank* • Federico García Lorca *Blood Wedding* • *Doña Rosita the Spinster* (bilingual edition) • *The House of Bernarda Alba* (bilingual edition) • *Yerma* (bilingual edition) • David Mamet *Glengarry Glen Ross* • *Oleanna* • Patrick Marber *Closer* • John Marston *The Malcontent* • Martin McDonagh *The Lieutenant of Inishmore* • *The Lonesome West* • *The Beauty Queen of Leenane* • Arthur Miller *All My Sons* • *The Crucible* • *A View from the Bridge* • *Death of a Salesman* • *The Price* • *After the Fall* • *The Last Yankee* • *A Memory of Two Mondays* • *Broken Glass* • Percy Mtwa, Mbongeni Ngema and Barney Simon *Woza Albert!* • Joe Orton *Loot* • Joe Penhall *Blue/Orange* • Luigi Pirandello *Six Characters in Search of an Author* • Lucy Prebble *Enron* • Mark Ravenhill *Shopping and F***ing* • Willy Russell *Blood Brothers* • *Educating Rita* • Sophocles *Antigone* • *Oedipus the King* • Wole Soyinka *Death and the King's Horseman* • Shelagh Stephenson *The Memory of Water* • August Strindberg *Miss Julie* • J. M. Synge *The Playboy of the Western World* • Theatre Workshop *Oh What a Lovely War* • Frank Wedekind *Spring Awakening* • Timberlake Wertenbaker *Our Country's Good* • Arnold Wesker *The Merchant* • Oscar Wilde *The Importance of Being Earnest* • Tennessee Williams *A Streetcar Named Desire* • *The Glass Menagerie* • *Cat on a Hot Tin Roof* • *Sweet Bird of Youth*